W9-BCR-412

DATE DUE

15.90

978.9   Thompson, Kathleen.
Tho
         New Mexico

PROPERTY OF
CHICAGO BOARD OF EDUCATION
DONALD L. MORRILL SCHOOL

STECK-VAUGHN

PORTRAIT OF AMERICA

New Mexico

Copyright © 1996 Steck-Vaughn Company   C.1 1997

All rights reserved. No part of this book may be reproduced or utilized in any form or by any means, electronic or mechanical, including photocopying, recording, or by any information storage and retrieval system, without permission in writing from the copyright owner. Requests for permission to make copies of any part of the work should be mailed to: Copyright Permissions, Steck-Vaughn Company, P.O. Box 26015, Austin, Texas 78755.

15.90

Steck-Vaughn Company

Executive Editor	Diane Sharpe
Senior Editor	Martin S. Saiewitz
Design Manager	Pamela Heaney
Photo Editor	Margie Foster
Electronic Cover Graphics	Alan Klemp

Proof Positive/Farrowlyne Associates, Inc.
Program Editorial, Revision Development, Design, and Production

Consultant: Michael E. Pitel, New Mexico Department of Tourism

Published by Raintree Steck-Vaughn Publishers, an imprint of Steck-Vaughn Company.

A Turner Educational Services, Inc. book. Based on the Portrait of America television series by R. E. (Ted) Turner.

Cover Photo: Santuario de Chimayo by © Cynthia Ellis.

Library of Congress Cataloging-in-Publication Data

Thompson, Kathleen.
   New Mexico / Kathleen Thompson.
      p.   cm. — (Portrait of America)
   "Based on the Portrait of America television series"—T.p. verso.
   "A Turner book."
   Includes index.
   ISBN 0-8114-7376-7 (library binding).—ISBN 0-8114-7457-7 (softcover)
      1. New Mexico—Juvenile literature. I. Title. II. Series:
   Thompson, Kathleen. Portrait of America.
   F796.3.T46 1996
   978.9—dc20   95-44445
                                                      CIP
                                                      AC

Printed and Bound in the United States of America

1 2 3 4 5 6 7 8 9 10 WZ 98 97 96 95

Acknowledgments
The publishers wish to thank the following for permission to reproduce photographs:
P. 7 © Superstock; p. 8 © Cynthia Ellis; p. 10 (top) © Cynthia Ellis, (bottom) © Jack Moehn Jr. /Profiles West; p. 11 Kansas State Historical Society; p. 12 Museum of New Mexico; p. 13 (top) © Mark Nohl/New Mexico Magazine, (bottom) Colorado Historical Society; p. 15 Kit Carson Historic Museum; p. 16 (both) © Cynthia Ellis; p. 17 (both) Museum of New Mexico; p. 19 © Mark Nohl/New Mexico Magazine; p. 21 © Mark Gibson/Profiles West; pp. 22, 23 Los Alamos National Laboratory; p. 24 Intel Corporation; pp. 26, 27 © Mark Nohl/New Mexico Magazine; pp. 28, 29 Ortega's Weaving Shop; p. 30 © Merilyn Brown; p. 31 Ortega's Weaving Shop; p. 32 Museum of New Mexico; p. 33 Elephant Butte Irrigation District; p. 34 © Christopher Acque/Institute of American Indian Arts Museum; p. 37 Metropolitan Museum of Art, Stieglitz Collection; p. 38 (top) © Mark Nohl/New Mexico Magazine, (bottom) © Tim Haske/Profiles West; p. 39 (top) © Bob Lienemann/Profiles West, (bottom) Carlsbad Caverns National Park; p. 40 Institute of American Indian Arts Museum; p. 41 © Cynthia Ellis; p. 42 © Phil Lauro/Profiles West; p. 44 © Cynthia Ellis; p. 46 One Mile Up; p. 47 (top left) Texas Highways Magazine, (top right) © Mark Nohl/New Mexico Magazine, (bottom) One Mile Up.

STECK-VAUGHN

PORTRAIT OF AMERICA

New Mexico

Kathleen Thompson

A Turner Book

RSVP

**RAINTREE
STECK-VAUGHN**
PUBLISHERS
The Steck-Vaughn Company

Austin, Texas

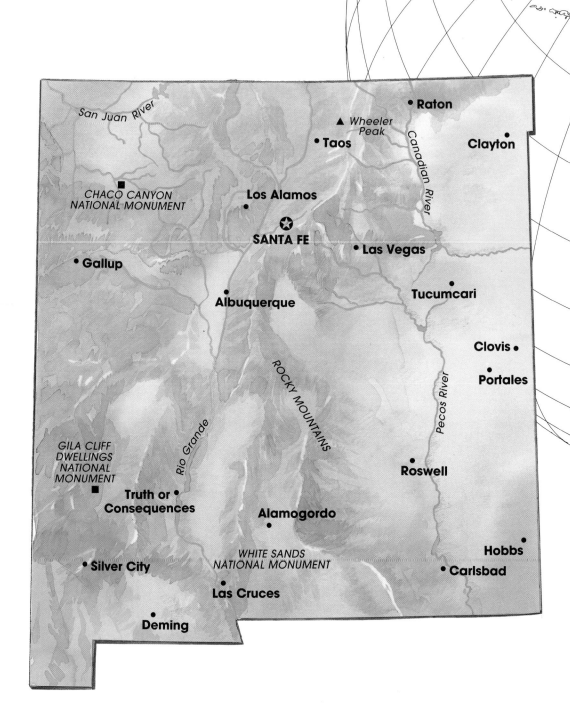

New Mexico

San Juan River

▲ Wheeler Peak

• Raton

• Taos

Clayton

■ CHACO CANYON NATIONAL MONUMENT

Canadian River

• Los Alamos

⭐ **SANTA FE**

• Las Vegas

• Gallup

Tucumcari

Albuquerque

Clovis •

• Portales

ROCKY MOUNTAINS

Pecos River

Rio Grande

GILA CLIFF DWELLINGS NATIONAL MONUMENT

• Roswell

■ Truth or Consequences

Alamogordo

Hobbs •

• Silver City

WHITE SANDS NATIONAL MONUMENT

• Carlsbad

Las Cruces

• Deming

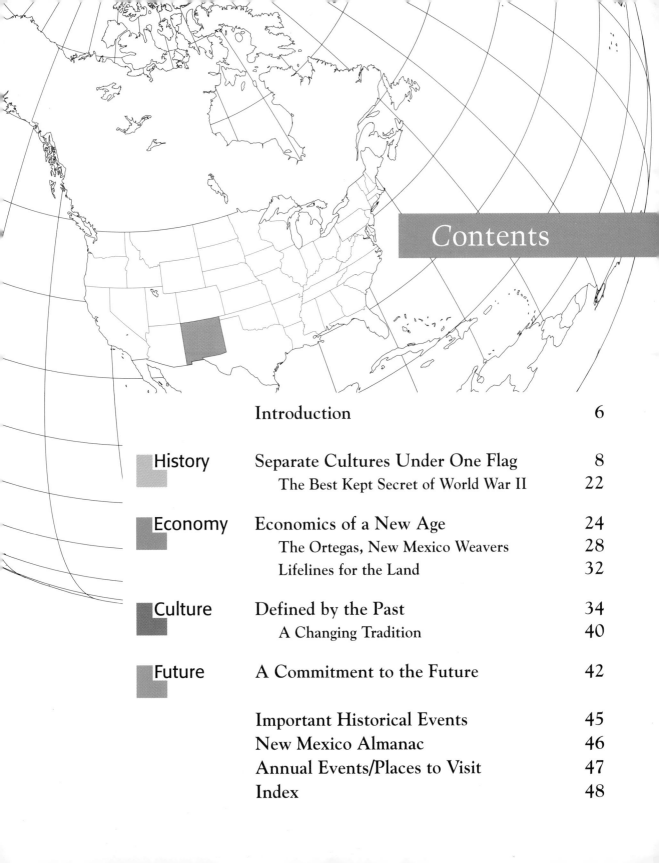

Contents

Introduction

New Mexico, the "Land of Enchantment," is a place of beauty and mystery. Nature has graced it with blooming deserts, snow-crested mountains, and rocks sculpted by wind and water. The sun paints it with vivid colors—red-brown land against sparkling blue sky, and the golds and purples of dusk and dawn. New Mexico's people are no less surprising. Early inhabitants constructed wonderful towns of rock and then mysteriously abandoned them. The Spaniards first tried to overcome the native cultures in New Mexico and then learned to live with the Native Americans. Settlers from the eastern United States added their own pioneering culture to the blend. The result is a state that makes use of today's science and technology while respecting its own natural wonders and rich traditional heritage.

The Taos Pueblo, shown here, displays the cultural heritage that makes New Mexico so unique. The Pueblo have lived at Taos Pueblo for more than one thousand years.

adobe, Navajo, acequias

Separate Cultures Under One Flag

For as long as 12,000 years, people have lived in New Mexico. This region was home to several early cultures, including one of the greatest in North America. This particular group is known by the ruins of their well-built villages. The Navajo named them the *Anasazi*, meaning "the ancient ones." The Anasazi grew crops and made beautiful pottery and jewelry. They built a network of *pueblos*, or settlements. The pueblos in Chaco Canyon were home to about seven thousand people!

Around A.D. 1300 the Anasazi began to break up into smaller groups. These groups became part of the Native American group we now call the Pueblo. The Zuni and the Hopi are Pueblo groups descended from the Anasazi.

The New Mexico region was also home to the Ute, the Comanche, and three Apache groups—Jicarilla, Mescalero, and Chiricahua. The Ute lived in the mountains and plains of northern New Mexico. The Ute lived in either homes made of grass and reeds

This kiva is part of the ancient Anasazi settlement at Chaco Canyon. A kiva is a round chamber used for religious ceremonies. The walls of this kiva were homes for the Anasazi .

These petroglyphs, or pictures carved in rock, were an early form of writing. They were left here by prehistoric people thousands of years ago.

or cone-shaped teepees covered with buffalo skin. They hunted antelope, buffalo, and elk and collected berries, nuts, and roots.

The Comanche lived in many areas of the western lands, including New Mexico. They were mainly nomads, which means they moved often and lived in temporary villages. They were a warrior society that survived mainly by hunting buffalo and raiding other groups.

The Apache were also nomads. They hunted buffalo and other game and gathered wild plants for food. By 1500 the Navajo had moved into present-day New Mexico. The Navajo were warriors who lived in permanent villages. The Pueblo taught them how to grow crops.

In 1528 Spanish explorer Álvar Nuñez Cabeza de Vaca and three others survived a shipwreck off the coast of present-day Texas. After eight years spent exploring areas of the Southwest, the group made their

The Gila Cliff Dwellings were built around 1200. Now a historic monument, they were once the site of a Pueblo settlement.

During their travels Francesco Vásquez de Coronado and his soldiers thought they had discovered one of the Seven Cities of Cíbola. However, it turned out to be the pueblo at Ácoma Rock, southwest of present-day Albuquerque.

way to a Spanish settlement in Mexico. They told stories about cities of gold called the Seven Cities of Cíbola. About 1540 Father Marcos de Niza, a Catholic priest, had Cabeza de Vaca's former slave Estevanico guide him to the golden cities. When the group reached present-day New Mexico, the Zuni resisted their progress, and the group returned to Mexico. A few years later, Father de Niza accompanied Francisco Vásquez de Coronado on his search for the Seven Cities of Cíbola. Coronado also encountered the Zuni, but he was not turned back like the earlier expedition had been. Coronado's troops killed almost everyone in one of the Zuni villages.

Coronado explored the area for two years, finally turning back after reaching the Grand Canyon. He claimed the region for Spain. In 1598 Juan de Oñate established San Juan de los Cabelleros, the first Spanish colony in present-day New Mexico. Oñate invaded Pueblo villages and either killed the Pueblo or took them into slavery. The colony did not thrive. In 1610 the governor of Mexico replaced Oñate with Pedro de Peralta.

Diego de Vargas was the governor of the province of New Mexico toward the end of the seventeenth century.

One of Peralta's first acts was to move the capital closer to the Pueblo villages. He named the new capital La Villa Real de la Santa Fe, known today as Santa Fe. Peralta's government forced the Pueblo to pay taxes of food and supplies and to work for the Spanish. Missionaries demanded that the Pueblo stop worshipping their gods and convert to Christianity. Finally, in 1680 a Pueblo named El Popé led a revolt against the Spanish. More than four hundred Spaniards were killed. The rest fled to El Paso in present-day Texas.

In 1692 the Spanish returned to Santa Fe. After four years of fighting, the Spanish forces led by Diego de Vargas defeated the Pueblo. This time the Spanish made land grants to the Pueblo, giving them the freedom to farm. In addition the missionaries showed more tolerance of the Pueblo religion. Peace allowed new Spanish and Pueblo settlements to begin.

In the early 1700s, Albuquerque and other settlements were founded in the New Mexico area. For the next eighty years, both Pueblo and Spanish settlements were attacked by raiding parties of Apache, Navajo, and Comanche warriors. Settlement slowed during this period, as few people wanted to come to such a dangerous region. In 1778 Juan Bautista de Anza became governor of the province of New Mexico. It took him almost ten years to defeat the Comanche and have them sign a peace treaty. After that the Comanche fought on the side of the Spanish against the Apache and the Navajo.

Events far to the east had a major effect on the New Mexico area in the late 1700s and early 1800s.

These Pueblo are performing a ceremonial cloud dance in Pojoaque.

The United States won its independence from Great Britain in 1783. In 1803 the United States bought the Louisiana Territory from France for $15 million. That territory included the land between the Mississippi River and the Rocky Mountains. In 1806 Zebulon M. Pike was sent westward by General James Wilkinson, the governor of the Louisiana Territory, to explore the new territory. Pike and his men became lost, and in 1807 they camped on a branch of the Rio Grande in present-day New Mexico. Pike was arrested by Spanish troops, who accused him of spying. He was released after questioning. Pike's travels resulted in valuable maps of the New Mexico region.

The Spanish did not allow any trade with the United States. They feared that American traders would gain too much power in the sparsely populated region. In 1821 Mexico won its independence from

Zebulon Pike's written reports about the Southwest attracted American fur traders and trappers to the area.

Spain, and the New Mexico region became a province of Mexico. The Mexican government removed trade restrictions with Americans. That same year William Becknell, an American trader, opened a trade route known as the Santa Fe Trail. The trail ran westward from Independence, Missouri, across Kansas to the Arkansas River. The Mountain Fork continued west along the Arkansas River, turning south through Raton Pass. The Cimarron Fork ran southwest through plains country. The Cimarron Fork was shorter and became the more popular route despite unfriendly Native Americans and a lack of water.

In 1845 the United States added the Republic of Texas to the Union. Part of this land was today's New Mexico. Mexico still claimed to own the republic even though Texas had declared its independence from Mexico ten years earlier. The result of the dispute was the Mexican War. Early in the war, General Stephen W. Kearny captured Santa Fe without bloodshed. Kearny established a civil government with Charles Bent, a Santa Fe trader, as governor. General Sterling Price was in charge of military control of New Mexico. In 1847 the Mexicans rebelled against the American occupation. Bent was murdered at his home in Taos. General Price fought three battles with rebels and brought the revolt under control. The Mexican War ended in 1848, with the United States gaining most of what is now New Mexico, California, Utah, Nevada, and Arizona, as well as parts of Colorado and Wyoming.

In 1850 New Mexico became a United States territory. This territory included all or part of present-day Arizona, Colorado, Nevada, and Utah. During the 1850s the question of slavery was a national issue. Members of Congress representing the South and the North were evenly divided on the issue. Southern states wanted new territories to accept slavery as a condition of statehood. Northern states opposed slavery. In 1848 New Mexicans voted that slavery would be illegal in the territory. The territory expanded with the Gadsen Purchase of 1853 when the United States bought the southernmost parts of Arizona and New Mexico from Mexico.

In 1861, 11 Southern states seceded, or broke away, from the Union, establishing the Confederate States of America. Slavery and states' rights were the main reasons for the split. President Abraham Lincoln tried unsuccessfully to bring the two sides together peacefully, but he could not prevent the start of the Civil War later that year. Almost immediately, Confederate forces from Texas invaded New Mexico and captured Albuquerque and Santa Fe. The Confederates hoped to use western silver and gold to finance the war. They also wanted to gain control of the West to have access to California ports. In 1862 the New Mexicans defeated the Texans in a decisive battle at Glorieta Pass.

During the Civil War, the biggest threat to New Mexicans was not the Confederacy. It was the Apache and the Navajo, who had renewed their raids on settlements. The New Mexicans fought back, destroying Native American villages, fields, and orchards. During the Civil War, Kit Carson served as a colonel of the

Before the Civil War, Kit Carson lived in Taos and served as the United States agent to the Utes.

A mining rush in the late 1800s brought many settlers to New Mexico, but most of them never struck it rich. This photo shows an abandoned mining house.

Lincoln Tower is a historic rock fort that has been preserved as a remembrance of the Lincoln County War.

New Mexico volunteers. He also was called on to fight the Navajo and the Apache, whom he helped defeat. The Native Americans were forced to move onto Bosque Redondo reservation in the southeast. Many Navajo died during the journey, which has become known among Native Americans as the "Long Walk."

The Bosque Redondo was a dry, barren land, and hundreds died there. In 1865 the Apache left the reservation and began fighting for the return of their homeland. In 1868 the federal government gave the Navajo a large reservation in their old homeland in return for the Navajo's promise to end their raids on American settlements. Soon the Jicarilla and Mescalero Apache moved to their old homeland, now a reservation in the Sacramento Mountains. Only the Chiricahua, led by Cochise, Geronimo, and Mangas Coloradas, continued to fight.

After the Civil War ended in 1865, more settlers moved into New Mexico territory. Cattle and sheep ranching thrived. Texas ranchers drove their herds through New Mexico to railroads in the north. Gold had been discovered at Pinos Altos in 1860, and miners swept over the mountains, establishing mining towns. After 1866 town after town sprang up almost overnight.

Feuds arose between cattle ranchers and sheepherders in 1876. Both groups fought for control of grazing land in Lincoln County. Several skirmishes involving stolen sheep and cattle turned to violence. The feud, called the Lincoln County War, ended when General Lew Wallace was appointed territorial governor. He rounded up the main troublemakers and helped negotiate a peace.

New Mexico became linked to the rest of the United States in 1881, with the completion of the southern transcontinental railroad from Kansas City to Los Angeles. The railroad passed through the New Mexico communities of Raton, Las Vegas, Albuquerque, Socorro, and Deming.

Land ownership became a source of conflict between the Spanish settlers, or Hispanics, and the Americans, or Anglos, during this time. The Hispanics had a tradition of giving blocks of land to entire communities. Anyone in the community could use the land for grazing or growing crops. The Anglos, however, had a different tradition. Individuals considered the land they were on their own, and no one else could use it. This caused many problems when the territorial government tried to pass laws involving land

Billy the Kid was a member of a special posse that took part in the Lincoln County War.

The Atchison, Topeka, and Santa Fe Railroad, which began running in 1878, brought many new settlers to New Mexico.

ownership and property rights. Finally, the territorial government divided the community-owned land into parcels and gave each individual in a community a parcel. There were many more parcels than there were families, however. Anyone could purchase the unclaimed community land. The system wasn't fair to the Hispanics who had owned that land for more than two centuries. Many Anglo businessmen became wealthy. They bought the unclaimed community land at very low prices and sold it for a large profit.

In 1912 New Mexico became the forty-seventh state. Mining and cattle ranching were big business, and agriculture developed as a result of irrigation. The new state had a population of 330,000.

In 1916 Pancho Villa, a Mexican rebel, raided the New Mexico town of Columbus, just across the border. Villa was angry with President Woodrow Wilson for backing Mexican leader Venustiano Carranza. The rebels killed 16 people and fled back to Mexico. The United States Army followed Villa into Mexico, but he was not captured.

In the 1920s New Mexico suffered a drought. Ranchers couldn't feed their cattle, and many farmers lost their land and their savings. Many people left the state. The state's economy took a turn for the better in 1922 when oil was discovered in southeastern and northwestern New Mexico. The state also began mining potash for use in making fertilizers, soaps, and glass. In 1924 New Mexico's Native Americans were granted United States citizenship, although they wouldn't have the right to vote until 1947.

This oil pump belongs to one of New Mexico's many oil fields. Forty percent of the state's mining income comes from the oil industry.

New Mexico suffered the hardship of the Great Depression in the 1930s along with the rest of the United States. Banks closed their doors, and industries shut down. Many people lost their life savings. In 1932 another drought ravaged the land, especially in the eastern part of the state where most of the farms were located. The soil turned to dust. Winds whipped up dust clouds so high and thick that they blocked out the sun.

The United States entered World War II in 1941. Military weapons development and testing helped the state's economy during the war. Rocket research that the military was already doing in New Mexico's desert speeded up. Los Alamos was established as a scientific research community. In 1945 the first atomic bomb was exploded at Trinity Site in a remote area of New Mexico. A short time later, the United States dropped two atomic bombs on the Japanese cities of

Hiroshima and Nagasaki. Japan surrendered soon after, ending World War II.

The federal government built more research laboratories and test sites in New Mexico after the war. The government continued to purchase land throughout the 1950s. White Sands became an important missile-testing area. Sandia National Laboratories was a center for studying the uses of nuclear energy. The state's population grew quickly as workers came to fill government jobs. Between 1950 and 1960, New Mexico's population grew by thirty percent!

The 1950s and 1960s were also a time of growth in New Mexico's mineral industry. In 1950 Paddy Martinez, a Navajo, discovered uranium in northwestern New Mexico, and the state immediately began mining uranium. In the 1960s copper and coal mining began, and production of oil and natural gas increased. During this period some of the military bases started to shrink their operations. Population growth slowed to about seven percent.

In the 1970s people of retirement age began moving to New Mexico because of its dry climate and its clean air. The state also attracted private businesses. Many were high-tech companies that supplied computers and sophisticated tools for New Mexico's research centers. A system of dams and reservoirs on the state's rivers brought freshwater for irrigating farmland. During the 1970s New Mexico's population grew by about 28 percent.

Military research in New Mexico increased in the 1980s because the federal government was conducting

Albuquerque, New Mexico's largest city, is a thriving tourist destination as well as a transportation and commercial center.

research to build a satellite defense system. Research employment made up for a slowdown in mining industries. Many new American industries were established just across the border in Mexico. In 1993 Santa Teresa, New Mexico, became an official international port of entry.

Today, New Mexico is an important center for space and nuclear research, mining, and tourism. Hispanics and Native Americans make up a large portion of the population, but they don't receive an equal share in the state's economy. The state's Native American, Hispanic, and Anglo populations form a rich, tricultural environment. The state has preserved many historical sites, and others continue to be part of everyday life. The rare and beautiful landscape known to the early Native Americans and the Spanish and the American settlers remains for the enjoyment and use of all New Mexico's residents today.

The Best Kept Secret
of World War II

An atomic bomb blast such as this one was first set off at Trinity Site.

In the early years of World War II, many scientists believed it was possible to split the nucleus, or positively charged center, of a uranium atom. They believed the huge quantity of energy released by such a reaction could be used to make a bomb more powerful than anyone could imagine. The United States government called upon American scientists to control this atomic power before its enemy, Germany, could do so.

By 1940 some of the best scientific minds in the world had begun developing an atomic bomb. They called their effort the Manhattan Project because some of the research had been conducted at Columbia University in Manhattan. To maintain the secrecy of the project and to be near testing sites, the scientists moved to the isolated site of Los Alamos, New Mexico.

People in the area were aware that scientists were working at Los Alamos, but the Manhattan Project remained a secret. In 1945 Germany surrendered, but the United States was still at war with Germany's ally Japan. Scientists were ready to test their first atomic bomb as soon as they could find a test site.

Alamogordo Air Base, about 120 miles south of Los Alamos, met the requirements for a test site because it was flat and unpopulated. Shortly before dawn on July 16, 1945, scientists set off the bomb. The explosion began with an intense flash of light. Next, a giant fireball rose into the sky. Following the fireball came a mushroom-shaped cloud that extended forty thousand feet. The desert sand surrounding the area melted into a glassy substance. People for miles around saw and felt the explosion. Because the country was at war, however, the public was not told exactly what had occurred. One month later the United States dropped atomic bombs on two Japanese cities, Hiroshima and Nagasaki. Japan surrendered after the second bombing.

Today, thousands of people live in Los Alamos. Many of them work at Los Alamos National Laboratory. They conduct research and use their understanding of nuclear science to make medical and scientific discoveries.

In the early 1990s, students in New Mexico read about a statue in Hiroshima Peace Park commemorating those who died in the bombing. They decided to erect a peace statue in Los Alamos. The statue was designed and planned by young people, and it has support from children all over the world. The statue symbolizes young people's vision of world peace.

J. Robert Oppenheimer led the group of scientists that organized the efforts of the Manhattan Project.

Economics of a New Age

For New Mexico's economy to thrive, all of its citizens must work together to use scarce resources as efficiently and responsibly as possible. Because New Mexico gets so little rain, agriculture has never been as strong here as in other states. New Mexico only has about seven thousand farms, most of which cover less than one hundred acres. Cattle are New Mexico's chief agricultural product. Sheep and wool are also important. Cattle ranches and sheep ranches cover millions of acres of land that is too dry for farming. The main field crop is hay, although farmers also grow cotton, grain sorghum, and wheat. New Mexico is a leading producer of chili peppers and pecans. Altogether agriculture produces two percent of New Mexico's economy.

Mining has always been part of New Mexico's economy. Gold and silver were mined by prospectors in the 1850s. These and other minerals are still mined in the state. For example New Mexico leads the nation in potash, a vital element in fertilizer. Workers also

Electronic products, such as this computer chip, are the most important goods manufactured in New Mexico.

Because New Mexico is so arid, farmers build irrigation ditches to bring water to their crops.

mine copper, gypsum, perlite, salt, sand, gravel, zinc, clay, and gemstones.

New Mexico supplies minerals that provide energy to the whole country. The state is one of the world's leading sources of uranium, the main source of nuclear energy. The most abundant energy products mined in the state are natural gas and petroleum, however. Mining brings in 12 percent of New Mexico's economy.

High-tech manufacturing industries have made their presence known in New Mexico. For example Albuquerque is home to companies such as Intel and Motorola, the country's largest manufacturers of computer chips and semiconductors. Honeywell produces communication systems for satellites. Plastics companies make products for medicine and communications. Companies in New Mexico also manufacture electrical equipment, food products, printed materials, and concrete. Manufacturing makes up nine percent of New Mexico's economy.

The federal government has been a part of New Mexico's economy since World War II. In fact most of the recent

growth in New Mexico's economy has resulted from federal government activity. Special research centers, such as the one at Los Alamos, study nuclear energy for both destructive and peaceful uses. There are also two important military facilities in the state, Kirtland Air Force Base and White Sands Missile Range. One out of every four people in the state works for the federal government.

The government is also an important part of New Mexico's service industry. In this industry people do not manufacture a product. Instead they may work as cooks, real estate agents, or doctors. The federal government employs service people to work in the national parks and to oversee programs on the Native American reservations. Altogether the service industry makes up 71 percent of New Mexico's economy.

New Mexico relies more heavily on high technology and services for its income today than in the past. The state still employs people in a variety of jobs, however. Given its contrasts, traditions, and commitment to the future, New Mexico's economy should improve with time.

Cattle ranches in New Mexico sometimes cover thousands of acres.

The Ortegas, New Mexico Weavers

Not many people in the United States can say that they live in the same place that their ancestors built almost three hundred years ago. That is the case with David Ortega, however. David Ortega's ancestors moved north from Mexico in the early 1700s and built their homes in Chimayo. The town is about 35 miles north of Santa Fe. It lies between the Jemez and Sangre de Cristo mountains. "This particular valley is very self-sufficient because we have water and you can grow almost anything here," said Ortega. "People who have any acreage at all can make a livelihood."

What did it mean to be self-sufficient in the early days? That may be difficult for some to imagine today. Most people can run to the mall or grocery store to pick up the items that they need. But in the 1700s, there were no malls or grocery stores. In fact there was very little contact between communities. If people needed something, they had to provide it themselves. People grew their own food, built their own homes, and wove their own blankets.

Mexican settlers such as the Ortegas brought the art of weaving to Chimayo. At first the Ortegas wove blankets only for themselves. When the railroads came to Chimayo in 1885, a little bit of civilization came,

David Ortega represents the sixth generation of weavers in his family.

28

too. Suddenly, items that had been difficult to obtain—canned goods, axes, pans, and other useful things—were available. In the early 1900s, Nicacio Ortega and his wife, Virginia, opened a general store in Chimayo.

Virginia was also a weaver, and the couple kept their weaving looms in the back of the store. They sold canned goods and farming supplies, and they also sold their blankets. Nicacio's business grew, and soon everyone in the

The interior of the weaving company owned by the Ortegas features weavings with the family's traditional patterns and designs.

In addition to their own weavings, the Ortegas also sell items that have been woven by other families in the Chimayo area.

family was producing weavings for the store.

Nicacio's sons David and Jose and their families joined the business in 1945. The Ortegas expanded their products to feature such items as woven purses, vests, rugs, and coats. As more and more people learned about the quality of the work and the lovely and unusual designs, the demand for the woven products by the Ortegas increased.

The Ortegas eventually discontinued selling the general merchandise. The store grew into the Ortegas' Weaving Shop. Even though Nicacio's sons and their families were working hard, they couldn't keep up with the demand for their weavings. In the 1950s the Ortegas decided to turn the family business into a cottage industry. The Ortegas supplied other weavers in Chimayo with looms and material and then sold the products in their shop. At times more than a hundred weavers were working regularly for the Ortegas.

Nicacio died in 1964, and Jose died in 1972. David and his wife, Jeannie, continued to run the business. Their sons Robert and Andrew added their own weaving skills. David's brother Medardo moved to the Old Town area in Albuquerque. He sells the Ortegas' products in his shop, which is called Ortegas' Old Town.

In 1980 Andrew and his wife, Evita, took over Jose's home and turned it into the Galeria Ortega, a showcase for New Mexican arts and crafts. Shoppers can find all the traditional Ortega weavings there, as well as such items as Hopi kachina dolls, pottery, and woodcarvings. Included in the Galeria are Andrew's loom and the work of Andrew's children, Katherine and Paul.

A few years ago, David Ortega retired. His son Robert now runs the Ortegas' Weaving Shop. In the back of the shop, visitors can watch weavers at work. The shop also sells pottery and jewelry produced by artisans in the nearby Pueblo villages.

The Ortegas are part of Chimayo. David Ortega explained it this way: "People have their roots here. . . . They don't sell the land. The people—the fathers and the mothers—hold their lands for their . . . grandchildren." Leaving home, breaking with tradition—that isn't the way of the Ortegas of Chimayo. They prefer to stay on the land they have called home for nearly three hundred years.

David Ortega (center) appears here with his sons Andrew (left) and Robert.

31

Lifelines for the Land

One thing that makes New Mexico a very special place is water—or the lack of it. The average rainfall in the state is only 13 inches per year, and some places get only 8 inches! Without water there is no life. New Mexicans have created a unique way to bring water to their land without counting on much rainfall. For over two hundred years, New Mexicans have used systems of narrow, shallow irrigation ditches called *acequias*.

These ditches, which run alongside community fields and gardens, use water diverted from a nearby river to irrigate the land.

An acequia begins at a river. Sometimes a dam is built to divert the water, and other times a channel is dug to make the water flow into the acequia. A main ditch may divide into several branches, but all branches come back to the acequia before it ends. Finally the acequia returns to the river farther downstream from where it began. In this way only part of the river is diverted, and people down-

Acequias are so important in New Mexico that in most communities, the acequias are built even before houses and other buildings are completed.

Building an acequia is hard work. The channels are dug with shovels and shaped with knives.

stream can build acequias from the river, too.

People do not use the water in the acequia for anything but irrigation. The acequia system belongs to those who use the water. It does not belong to the county or the state. That means the people who use it are the ones who must maintain it. An acequia must be kept clear of large rocks, tree limbs, and rubbish. Users elect a leader who is in charge of the acequia system, but the upkeep is a community responsibility. Users hold meetings to decide what needs to be done. It takes many people to keep these fragile streams of water clear and running.

The people whose families built these acequias understand that these ditches are important to the community. But some newcomers do not. They have to learn how to live in a land where water is precious. When people are used to modern technology, it is hard for them to realize how important it is to take care of a stream of water that may be less than two feet wide.

The acequias are an essential part of New Mexico culture because the water they bring represents life. John Nichols, a novelist who lives in Taos, puts it this way. "We want to live from the ground, from the earth. When the ditches are dry, everybody in the community feels discouraged because they can't see the water running." Land without water cannot bloom.

Defined by the Past

For some people the word *culture* means the fine arts—paintings, sculpture, classical music, literature, and theater. New Mexico has all of these things, especially in Santa Fe and Albuquerque. The Santa Fe Opera began in 1957. Its performances are still well-attended by New Mexicans and tourists from all over the United States. The opera presents its open-air performances in the Sangre de Cristo Mountains, just outside Santa Fe. The fine arts are also represented by the New Mexico Symphony Orchestra, which started in the 1930s. It was originally known as the Albuquerque Symphony. Every year Santa Fe sponsors the Santa Fe Chamber Music Festival. There are chamber music festivals in towns such as Angel Fire and Taos. New Mexico also has a number of art museums and art galleries that feature New Mexico artists.

Culture is also defined as an expression of a people's heritage. New Mexico's heritage comes from three distinct groups—Native Americans; Hispanics,

Each Pueblo village has its own distinctive pottery designs, often including geometric patterns.

who share a Spanish and a Mexican background; and English-speaking Americans, usually called Anglos.

Two groups of Native American people, the Pueblo and the Navajo, have made important contributions to New Mexico's culture. The Navajo are famous for their beautiful woven blankets and fine turquoise and silver jewelry. The Pueblo, besides being excellent pottery makers, also created a style of architecture that is still used throughout New Mexico and the Southwest. Many New Mexico buildings are built in the Pueblo style, made from a material called *adobe*. Adobe is a combination of clay, straw, and water. Adobe bricks make up the inner walls, which are then coated with an adobe plaster. The edges of the walls are rounded so that the corners are curved like those of a sand castle. Adobe is very durable. The combination of bricks and plaster holds the building firmly together as a unit. Adobe also soaks up the strong New Mexico sun and holds the warmth long after nightfall. There are some adobe homes in New Mexico that have been lived in for hundreds of years.

One of the most important contributions of Hispanics in New Mexico is the art of woodcarving. The most common objects are the carved figures of saints, known as *santos*. These figures are displayed in many of the fine old cathedrals that are still in use in many New Mexico towns and cities.

Anglos are responsible for bringing painting and European-style music, such as the opera, to New Mexico. Georgia O'Keeffe, one of the United States' most famous painters, lived much of her life in the state. She was inspired by the beauty and the vivid colors of the New Mexican landscape. In fact she chose to paint objects found in nature such as animal bones, flowers, and cliffs. Many Anglo artists and writers have come to "artist colonies" such as Taos to find inspiration in the beauty of New Mexico.

Fiestas, fairs, and dances are important expressions of New Mexico's culture. In late June the annual Mescalero Apache Indian Celebration is held in Ruidoso. The Pueblo sponsor the Puyé Cliff Ceremonial at Santa Clara Pueblo in July and the Green Corn Dance at Santo Domingo Pueblo in August.

Hispanics have also added much to the festival tradition. Fiestas such as the Feria Artesana in Albuquerque are festivals with food, entertainment, and arts and crafts. Albuquerque also hosts Luminaria Tours, a series of Christmas Eve bus tours that go past all the city's Christmas lights and luminarias, which are lit candles in sand-filled paper bags. In summer people travel to Santa Fe to see the Estampa Flamenca, a dance troupe that specializes in flamenco dancing. The burning of Zozobra is part of the Fiesta de Santa Fe. Zozobra, a two-story, papier-mâché monster that represents all the evil in the world, is paraded around

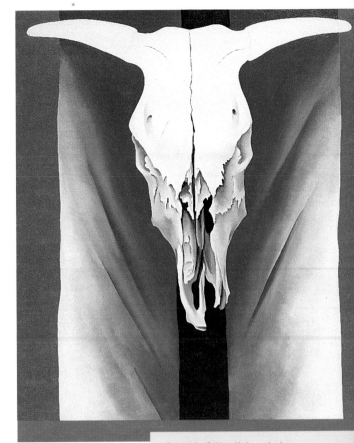

Georgia O'Keeffe's painting, "Cow's Skull: Red, White, and Blue," features the bleached skull and brilliant colors that are characteristic of many of her works.

This mariachi band is playing in the Fiesta de Santa Fe. Mariachis play Mexican folk music.

Visitors enjoy the natural exhibits at the Rio Grande Zoo.

in a great open field and lit afire at nightfall. The world's evil is carried away in the smoke and flames.

Other events in New Mexico include rodeos and various other celebrations of cowboy heritage. Professional and amateur theater are also very popular. In addition Albuquerque hosts the Kodak Albuquerque International Balloon Fiesta every October. Huge, colorful hot-air balloons from all over the world are brought to New Mexico for this event.

Exploring New Mexico culture can uncover a very deep past. For instance one of the most interesting places in New Mexico is Ácoma Pueblo, an ancient city that sits on top of a mesa more than 350 feet above the valley floor. People have lived in this pueblo for more than five thousand years. Ancient Native American villages and cave dwellings are also found throughout the state. What's more there are natural

Every October the Kodak Albuquerque International Balloon Fiesta attracts hundreds of hot-air balloon enthusiasts and thousands of spectators.

monuments to the past that stand as witnesses to the many changes that have occurred. These include the amazing rock formations carved by nature, such as the Bistra Badlands, the City of Rocks State Park, and Camel Rock outside Santa Fe.

The cultures of New Mexico are entwined by history. Many New Mexicans speak both English and Spanish, and people enjoy foods from each of the cultures. New Mexicans take part in all the festivals, regardless of their origin. Sharing creates a respect between cultures and preserves the contribution of each.

Carlsbad Caverns are a series of caves in southeastern New Mexico. They are considered to be one of the most awe-inspiring natural wonders in the world.

A Changing Tradition

For hundreds of years, the Navajo lived in the area that today includes parts of New Mexico, Arizona, and Utah. They learned sheepherding from the Spanish colonists and farming from the Pueblo. Navajo women spun sheep wool into yarn and used wild plant dyes to tint the yarn with soft, natural colors. They wove blankets and clothing using wooden looms.

The westward movement of American settlers in the mid-1800s disrupted the Navajo's lifestyle. When the United States Army built a fort on Navajo territory, clashes broke out between the Navajo and the soldiers. In 1863 United States Army troops defeated the Navajo and forced them to walk to a reservation 250 miles away. The Navajo spent five difficult years there before the government let them return to their homeland.

Much of the Navajo's land had been settled by others while they were away. The smaller area of land left for them to reclaim was not good for sheepherding or farming. American settlers had set up trading posts on

Navajo artists took up silversmithing in the late nineteenth century, and they quickly became masters at it. This is a turquoise and silver Navajo bracelet.

that land. The trading posts sold cooking pots, textiles, and food. The Navajo began trading their woven blankets and other goods in exchange for the items available at the trading posts. It turned out that people coming to the trading posts wanted to buy these Navajo goods, and the traders began selling them.

Although the Navajo had some experience working with silver, the traders hired Mexican silversmiths to refine their skills. Navajo men began reshaping silver coins into belt buckles, buttons, bracelets, and earrings. Eventually the Navajo began adding turquoise, an attractive blue stone found in the Southwest, to the jewelry. Silver and turquoise jewelry became a Navajo trademark.

Today, Navajo crafts are a unique blend of tradition and modern innovation. The rugs and blankets have kept their traditional Navajo pattern, but artificial dyes color them more brilliantly. Some Navajo jewelry still bears design elements, such as squash blossoms, which recall the Navajo farming tradition. Other popular designs have been created within the last few years.

Traditions sometimes must change. Navajo artists have achieved a balance between the old and the new.

This Navajo hogan is located in the town of Ghost Ranch. A hogan is a traditional Navajo house made of earth and logs.

A Commitment to the Future

New Mexico faces a number of issues that will have an impact on its future. Its minerals—oil, natural gas, coal, and uranium—provide energy resources for the country and jobs for the state. However, some minerals are located in unique places, such as the Anasazi ruins in Chaco Canyon. Mining for minerals in these areas could destroy ancient Native American artifacts. Also, these mineral resources could be used up.

Another issue for New Mexicans is the need for water. This has long been a problem in New Mexico and throughout the arid Southwest. New Mexico started building dams and reservoirs in 1908 and will likely build more in the future. All the industries that depend on this water are working together to recycle and conserve water as best they can. But water distribution is far from equal. High-tech companies such as Intel, a computer chip company in Albuquerque, require as much as nine million gallons of water every day! For New Mexico to attract high-tech industries, it will have to address the problem of limited water.

Albuquerque skyscrapers reach into the blue sky. Providing the water to support large industrial cities is a continuing challenge for New Mexico.

A rainbow arches over Orphan Mesa at Ghost Ranch. Rainbows are welcome sights in New Mexico's desert because they always follow a refreshing rain.

New Mexico is also looking for ways to have Hispanic and Native American citizens become more active in the economy. Community groups are turning their attention to improving the education system. The first goal is to lower the school dropout rate. Also, New Mexico's high-tech industries need well-educated workers, so businesses are working with educators and citizens by supporting technical schools and outreach programs.

The people of New Mexico understand that solving problems such as these will take patience and imagination. These changes will influence the everyday lives of New Mexico's citizens first. The economy of the state will be affected over a longer period of time. New Mexico enters the twenty-first century dedicated to improving the lives of its citizens both in the short term and also for a long time to come.

Important Historical Events

1300 The Anasazi break up and scatter into smaller groups, which become known as the Pueblo.

1400 Apache, Navajo, Ute, and Comanche begin arriving in present-day New Mexico.

1540 Father Marcos de Niza explores the New Mexico area.

1542 Francisco Vásquez de Coronado begins a two-year exploration and conquest of present-day New Mexico.

1598 *El Camino Real,* or the Royal Road, is completed, connecting the San Gabriel area with Chihuahua, Mexico. Juan de Oñate establishes San Juan de los Cabelleros, near the Chama River.

1610 Pedro de Peralta, governor of the colony, moves the capital to Santa Fe.

1680 The Pueblo drive the Spaniards out of the New Mexico area.

1692 Diego de Vargas, a Spanish governor, reconquers present-day New Mexico.

1706 Francisco Cuervo y Valdes founds Albuquerque.

1776 Silvestre de Escalante and Francisco Dominguez open the first leg of the Old Spanish Trail, which connects Santa Fe and Los Angeles, California.

1778 Juan Bautista de Anza becomes governor of the New Mexico province.

1821 Mexico wins its independence from Spain and makes the New Mexico area a Mexican province. Captain William Becknell opens the Santa Fe Trail.

1833 The first gold lode west of the Mississippi River is discovered at Sierra del Oro.

1845 The United States declares war on Mexico.

1846 General Stephen W. Kearny takes over present-day New Mexico.

1848 The Mexican War ends. Present-day New Mexico becomes part of the United States.

1853 The Gadsden Purchase adds the "bootheel" area to New Mexico.

1864 Colonel Kit Carson defeats the Navajo and the Mescalero Apache.

1876 Ranchers and other groups battle for control in the Lincoln County War.

1886 Geronimo surrenders to the United States Army.

1912 New Mexico becomes the forty-seventh state. The capital is Santa Fe.

1922 Large oil fields are discovered in San Juan County.

1930 Carlsbad Caverns National Park is created.

1945 The first atomic bomb is exploded at Trinity Site, near Alamogordo.

1962 The Navajo Dam is completed on the San Juan River.

1967 Hispanics revive a 120-year-land grant feud to reclaim land in an area included in the Carson National Forest.

1974 Jerry Apodaca is the first Hispanic elected governor since 1918.

1988 More than 1.4 million acres of land are damaged by drought and erosion.

1993 Santa Teresa becomes an official international port of entry between Mexico and New Mexico.

The New Mexico state flag is gold. In the center in red is the ancient sun symbol of the Zia Pueblo Native Americans.

New Mexico Almanac

Nickname. The Land of Enchantment

Capital. Santa Fe

State Bird. Roadrunner

State Flower. Yucca

State Tree. Piñon

State Motto. *Crescit Eundo* (It Grows as It Goes)

State Song. "O, Fair New Mexico"

State Abbreviations. N. Mex. or N.M. (traditional); NM (postal)

Statehood. January 6, 1912, the 47th state

Government. Congress: U.S. senators, 2; U.S. representatives, 3. State Legislature: senators, 42; representatives, 70. Counties: 33

Area. 121,593 sq mi (314,295 sq km), 5th in size among the states

Greatest Distances. north/south, 391 mi (629 km); east/west, 352 mi (566 km)

Elevation. Highest: Wheeler Park, 13,161 ft (4,011 m). Lowest: Red Bluff Reservoir, 2,817 ft (859 m)

Population. 1990 Census: 1,521,779 (17% increase over 1980), 37th among the states. Density: 11 persons per sq mi (4 persons per sq km). Distribution: 69% urban, 31% rural. 1980 Census: 1,299,968

Economy. *Agriculture:* beef cattle, cotton, milk, hay. *Manufacturing:* food products, electric and electronic equipment, printed materials, lumber and wood products. *Mining:* natural gas, petroleum, natural gas liquids, uranium, copper, potash

State Bird: Roadrunner

State Flower: Yucca

Annual Events

★ Winter Festival in Red River (January)

★ Dances, at most Native American pueblos (Easter)

★ Apache Indian Ceremonial in Mescalero (July 4)

★ "Billy the Kid" Pageant in Lincoln (early August)

★ Great American Duck Race in Deming (August)

★ New Mexico State Fair in Albuquerque (mid-September)

★ Taos Festival of the Arts (early October)

★ Kodak Albuquerque International Balloon Fiesta (October)

★ Navajo Fair in Shiprock (early October)

Places to Visit

★ Carlsbad Caverns National Park

★ Chaco Canyon

★ Gila Cliff Dwellings

★ Gila Wilderness

★ Los Alamos Bradbury Science Hall and Museum

★ Puyé Cliff Dwellings

★ San Miguel Mission

★ White Sands National Monument

State Seal

Index